THIS BOOK BELONGS TO

Wyatt

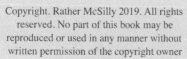

Q: What did one toilet say to the other toilet?

A: You look flushed.

Q: What stays in a corner and travels all over the world?

A: A stamp.

Q. What animal needs to wear a wig?

A: A bald eagle!

Q: What kind of shoes
do ninjas wear?

A: Sneakers!

Q: What is brown, hairy and wears sunglasses?

A: A coconut on vacation.

Q: What did one plate say to the other plate?

A: Dinner is on me!

Q: What did the Dalmatian say after lunch?

A: That hit the spot!

Q: Why was the baby strawberry crying?

A: Because her mom and dad were in a jam.

Q: What is worse than raining cats and dogs?

A: Hailing taxis!

Q: How do all the oceans say hello to each other?

A: They wave!

Q. What do you call a bear with no teeth?

A: A gummy bear!

Q: What do elves learn at school?

A: The elf-abet.

Q: What's a monster's favourite game?

A: Swallow the leader.

Q: What do you call a guy lying on your doorstep?

A: A Matt

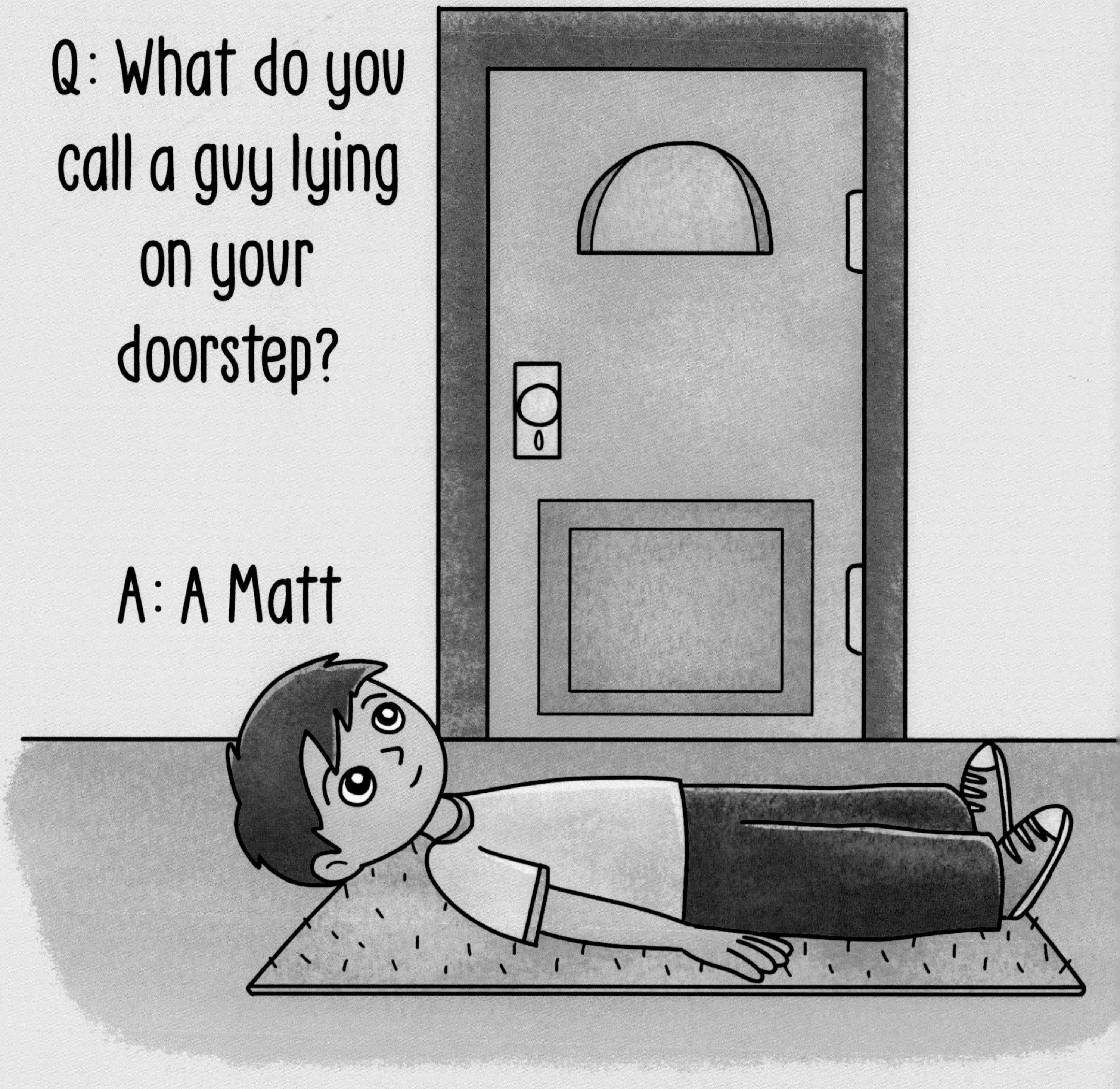

Q. What do you call a gorilla with bananas in its ears?

A: Anything you like, he can't hear you.

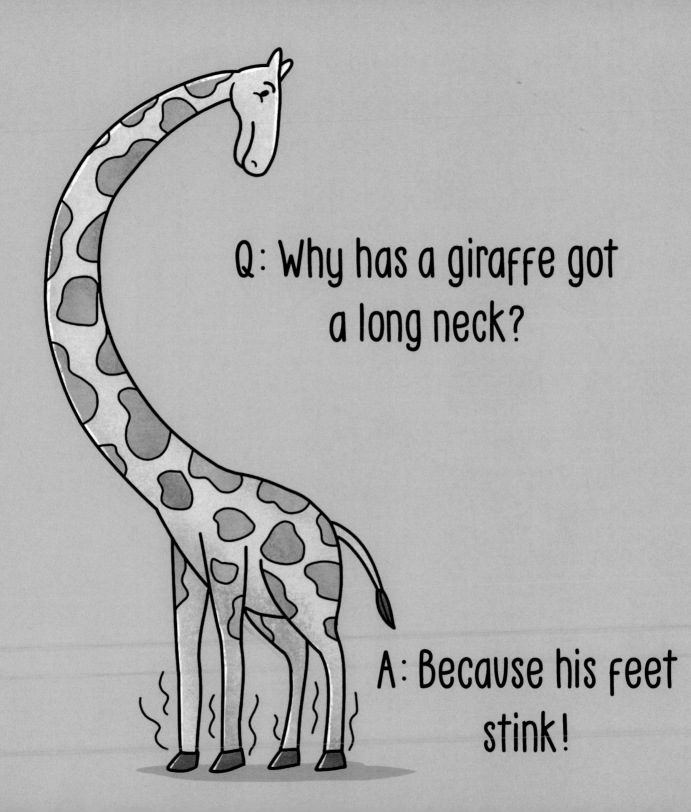

Q:Who was the first animal in space?

A: The cow that jumped over the moon.

Q: What did one volcano say to the other volcano

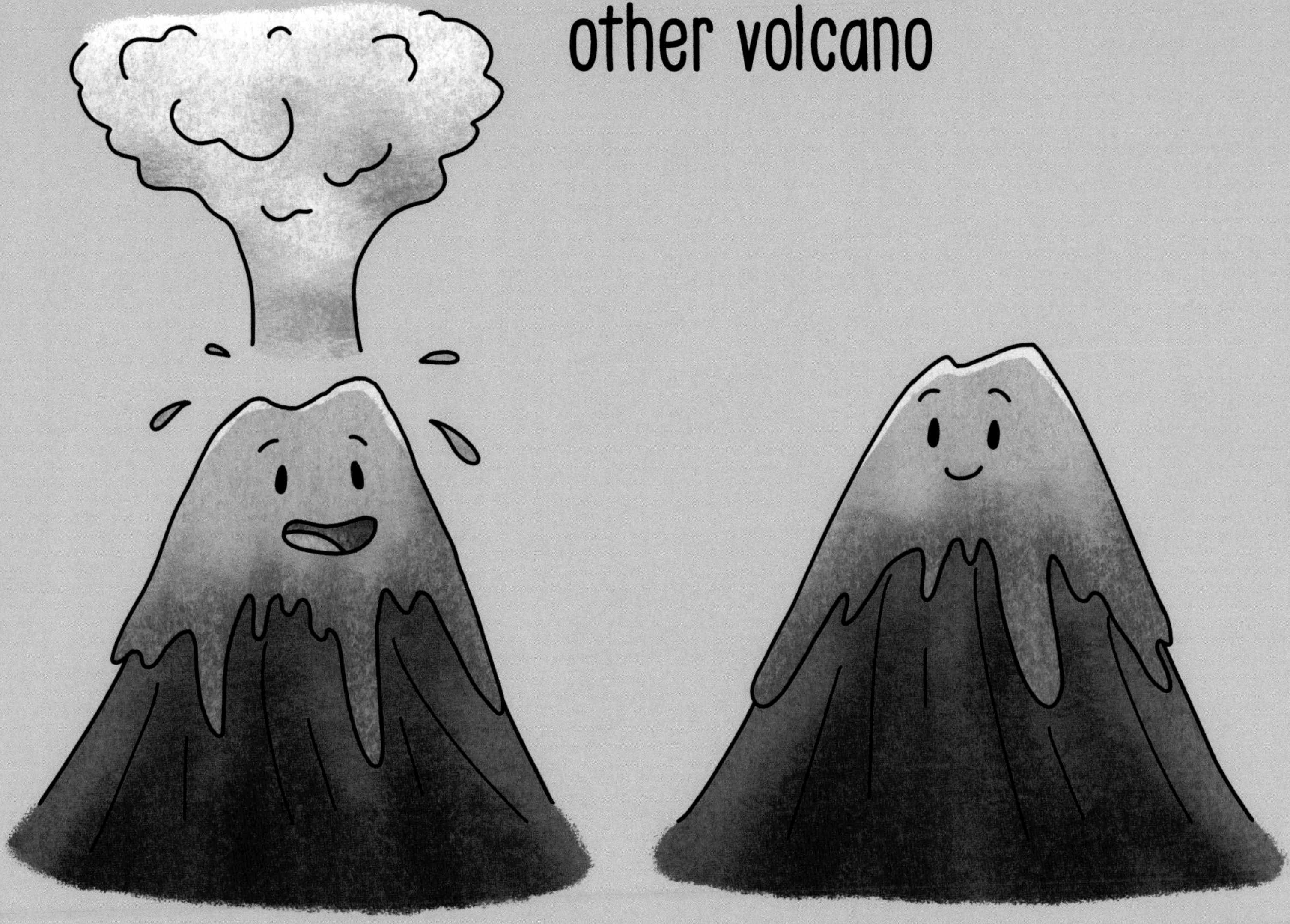

A: I lava you!

Q: Why did the jelly bean go to school?

A: Because he wanted to be a smartie.

Q: What is a rabbits favorite dance style?

A: Hip-Hop!

Q: What's a Koalas favorite drink?

A: Coca Koala!

Q: How do you ask a dinosaur to lunch?

A: Tea Rex?

Knock knock!

Who's there?

Donut

Donut who?

Donut ask me, I just got here.

Q: What's yellow and looks like pineapple?

A: A lemon with a new haircut.

Q: What did the baby corn ask mama corn?

A: Where's my pop corn?

If you have enjoyed this book of jokes, I ask you kindly to please leave a review on Amazon. It has a significant impact on independent artists, authors & businesses.

Thank you so much !